21st
Century
Skills Library

ANIMAL INVADERS

AUSTRALIAN SPOTTED JELLYFISH

SUSAN H. GRAY

Published in the United States of America by
Cherry Lake Publishing, Ann Arbor, Michigan
www.cherrylakepublishing.com

Content Adviser
Dr. Sarah Simons, Executive Director, Global Invasive Species Programme

Credits
Photos: Cover and pages 1 and 12, ©Dreamphoto1000 (Cathy Figuli)/
Dreamstime.com; page 4, ©John Carleton, used under license from Shutterstock,
Inc.; page 6, ©Mikhail Malyshev, used under license from Shutterstock, Inc.;
page 8, ©Rafael Ramirez Lee, used under license from Shutterstock, Inc.; page 11,
©iStockphoto.com/coleong; page 13, ©Ervphotos/Dreamstime.com; page 15, ©Olivier
Le Queinec, used under license from Shutterstock, Inc.; page 17, ©Francesco Ridolfi/
Alamy; page 18, ©Korosy/Dreamstime.com; pages 20 and 24, ©iStockphoto.com/
tshortell; page 22, ©ARCTIC IMAGES/Alamy; page 27, ©Francesco Ridolfi/Alamy

Map by XNR Productions Inc.
Please note: Our map is as up-to-date as possible at the time of publication.

Library of Congress Cataloging-in-Publication Data
Gray, Susan Heinrichs.
  Australian spotted jellyfish / by Susan H. Gray.
    p. cm.—(Animal invaders)
  Includes bibliographical references and index.
  ISBN-13: 978-1-60279-628-7
  ISBN-10: 1-60279-628-9
  1. Australian spotted jellyfish—Juvenile literature. 2. Marine
biological invasions—Juvenile literature. I. Title.
  QL377.S4G726 2010
  593.5'3—dc22   2009024168

Cherry Lake Publishing would like to acknowledge
the work of The Partnership for 21st Century Skills.
Please visit *www.21stcenturyskills.org* for more information.

Printed in the United States of America
Corporate Graphics Inc.
January 2010
CLSP06

ANIMAL INVADERS

TABLE OF CONTENTS

CHAPTER ONE
A FISH DINNER

The Australian spotted jellyfish (*Phyllorhiza punctata*) sinks gracefully in the ocean's warm water. A tiny, newly hatched fish brushes by. Its touch is gentle, but it triggers a deadly reaction. Stinging cells on the jellyfish's body burst

*Australian spotted jellyfish
are interesting creatures.*

open. They release tightly coiled threads that shoot toward the fish. Barbed points at the end of the threads pierce the fish's head and side. The fish struggles to get away. Within seconds, it is drawn beneath the jelly's umbrella. It is paralyzed by the poisoned barbs and will soon be digested.

LIFE & CAREER SKILLS

Many animals have misleading names. For example, jellyfish and starfish are not actually fish. Seahorses are not horses. And sea lions are certainly not lions. Often, scientists try to correct these names by creating new and more accurate ones. Jellyfish are one example. Scientists now prefer to call these animals sea jellies. Sometimes the new names catch on. Often, however, people stick with the old, familiar names. Do you think the new names make a difference? Would you encourage people to use them?

CHAPTER TWO
A DOUBLE LIFE

The Australian spotted jellyfish is a member of a group of animals called **cnidarians**. All cnidarians live in water, are soft-bodied, and have stinging cells. Sea jellies and sea **anemones** are cnidarians. So are the small, soft animals that create coral reefs.

Sea jellies are closely related to sea anemones.

Like many other cnidarians, the Australian spotted jellyfish has two body forms. These are the **polyp** and the **medusa**. As the jellies mature, they grow from one form into another. A polyp begins as a **larva**. What is a larva? Adult male jellies produce sperm cells. Females produce egg cells. When the sperm and eggs unite, they create a larva. The larva usually drifts to the sea floor and attaches to a rock or shell. Sometimes the larva brushes against the side of a ship and attaches there. No matter where it lands, the larva quickly develops into a polyp.

A polyp has a smooth, stalk-shaped body. There is a circle of short tentacles around the top. As it ages, its stalk begins to change. It doesn't stay smooth. Instead, it comes to look like a stack of saucers. In time, the top "saucer" pulls away and begins to swim. As it grows, it develops the umbrella-shaped body of an adult jelly, or medusa. Eventually, the remaining "saucers" also swim away and grow into adult jellies.

Most people are familiar with the dome-shaped medusa. It has long tentacles that drop gracefully from a transparent or faintly colored umbrella. Gentle, pulsing waves move through its body. These waves enable it to swim. The Australian spotted jellyfish medusa is brown or bluish brown with many small, white dots. The umbrella-shaped part is called a bell. In an adult it is usually about 18 inches (46 centimeters) across. The jelly's mouth area is on the underside of the bell. As the animal swims, water flows into this area. It then passes through a simple digestive system that traps nutrients. A jelly's food includes tiny floating animals called **zooplankton**. It also eats fish eggs, fish larvae, and even some other jellies. In a 24-hour period, more than 13,000 gallons (49,000 liters) of water can flow through the body of this animal.

The medusa has a simple nervous system. It has no brain. It has a network of nerves with sensors that detect light and shadows. The muscle system is also simple. A ring of muscle

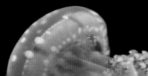

Sea jellies are very simple animals.

tissue encircles the body. As the muscles tense and ease, the bell squeezes and relaxes. This allows the jelly to move up and down in the water. It depends on waves and currents to move sideways.

LEARNING & INNOVATION SKILLS

Australian spotted jellyfish are actually clear to white in color. Their brown or bluish brown appearance comes from **algae** growing inside their bodies. These algae are helpful to the jellies.

Like plants, algae use sunlight to produce food and to grow. The jelly also uses this food for its own growth and nutrition. In return, the jelly's transparent body protects the algae while letting in plenty of sunshine. This is called a **symbiotic** relationship—two **organisms** living closely together. In the case of the algae and jelly, both organisms benefit. Can you think of other symbiotic relationships among plants or animals?

Like other jellies, the Australian spotted jellyfish has stinging cells on its body. Inside the cells are long, coiled, hair-like structures that end in sharp points. The cells spring open when a small fish or other **prey** brushes up against them. The hair-like structures shoot out, piercing the prey. Poison flows into the animal and paralyzes it. The poison of some jellies is so powerful that it can sicken or even kill a human being. The poison of the Australian spotted jellyfish, however, is weak. These jellies do not pose a threat to swimmers.

LEARNING & INNOVATION SKILLS

The animals that normally live in a particular area are called native **species**. Those that have been brought in from other areas are called non-native or introduced species. Thousands of species have been introduced to North America and its waters. Some cause damage to the environment or harm native species. When they cause problems, introduced animals are called **invasive** species.

Fortunately, not all introduced animals become invasive. Some prove beneficial. Brahman cattle, for example, were introduced to places around the world from India. They provide meat and can tolerate hot weather better than other types of cattle. Can you think of other introduced animals that have not become pests? How are they beneficial?

Australian spotted jellyfish are native to the east coast of Australia and other areas.

Australian spotted jellyfish are native to areas in the western Pacific Ocean. Scientists first described their presence along the coast of eastern Australia in 1884. Later, they reported the jellyfish in northern Australia and Thailand.

In recent years, scientists have seen the jellies near Western Australia, the Philippines, Hawaii, Brazil, and Puerto Rico. The jellies have also been seen in the Mediterranean Sea, the Gulf of Mexico, and along the eastern coastline of the United States. The jellies probably did not drift into these new areas on their own. Their spread is probably because of human activity.

CHAPTER THREE
SPREADING JELLY

The Australian spotted jellyfish began appearing in North American waters in the 1980s and 1990s. During those years, the jellies were occasionally seen in California and Louisiana.

The Australian spotted jellyfish's spots give it a unique appearance.

Since then, much larger populations have been found near Puerto Rico and in the Gulf of Mexico. This is thousands of miles from their natural home. The jellies prefer warm, coastal waters. The waters of the open ocean are cold. It is not likely that they drifted across thousands of miles of cold water to reach their new homes. How did they travel this great distance?

21ST CENTURY CONTENT

A number of invasive species have been carried around the world in ballast water. Scientists in many countries are working on ways to reduce the problem. One solution is to filter ballast water before it is released. Other solutions include killing the organisms in ballast water by using electric currents, heat, or poisons. None of these options is a perfect solution. What problems might arise with some of these methods? Can you think of ways to avoid those issues?

They probably traveled aboard ships when they were just tiny polyps or young medusae. Cargo ships draw seawater into their hulls before they leave port. The water serves as **ballast**. It weighs the ship down. The extra weight helps it stay balanced and avoid tipping over. The ballast water is loaded with all sorts of things—algae, young fish, larval clams, and little jellies. When a ship reaches its destination, it dumps the ballast. Often, the creatures in the ballast water survive the trip. Sometimes, conditions where they are dumped are similar to those in their native waters. If so, the released plants and animals thrive and reproduce.

Cargo ships play a role in spreading invasive species throughout the world's oceans.

Polyps might also travel another way. Normally, they attach to hard surfaces on the bottom of the sea floor. They land on rocks or shells and quickly cement themselves in place. But polyps can also attach to the outside of a ship's hull.

Ships often sit in a harbor for days or even weeks. It takes time to unload cargo and prepare for the next trip. During this time, snails, mussels, polyps, and other animals can attach to their hulls. Tiny, drifting zooplankton become entangled in seaweed strands dangling from anchors. When the ships depart, they take all of these plants and animals with them. Once the ships reach the next port, they spend several days being unloaded and prepared again. During that time, some animals might lay eggs. Polyps might produce little medusae. Seaweed might break off and begin to grow new strands. That's how populations of plants and animals, including the Australian spotted jellyfish, can develop where none existed before.

LIFE & CAREER SKILLS

The hull, or outside, of a ship is said to be **fouled** when plants and animals attach to it. For years, few people connected hull fouling to invasive species. Most scientists assumed that aquatic invaders traveled only in ballast water.

Then some scientists began to look more closely at fouled hulls. They found that millions of organisms could be riding on the hull of a single ship. These new observations made many people change their minds. Now some experts believe that fouled hulls carry more invaders than ballast water does. How do you think this new theory will affect human efforts to control aquatic invaders?

When jellies find their way to a new location, it is difficult to get rid of them.

CHAPTER FOUR
WHAT'S THE PROBLEM?

Australian spotted jellyfish are slow-moving, graceful animals. Unlike some jellies, their stings are very weak. They are not quick to attack. They do not chase after other animals. So why should anyone care that they are spreading?

Some kinds of sea jellies can cause painful stings.

One reason is that these jellies create problems for people who fish. Crews on large fishing ships drop huge nets into the ocean. As their ships move slowly along, the nets trap all sorts of fish, shrimp, and crabs. Jellies, however, can clog these nets. This makes them difficult to pull along. Some Australian spotted jellies weigh as much as 25 pounds (11 kilograms). Their large bodies block the flow of water through the nets. They also weigh the nets down. This reduces a ship's catch and can damage the nets. When the nets are hauled in, the crew must begin the slow task of untangling the trapped jellies.

These animals are also big eaters. The jellies feed constantly. Thousands of gallons of nutrient-rich water pass through their bodies every day. It doesn't take them long to devour all the fish eggs and larvae in an area. This can quickly wipe out fish populations. The jellies also eat a lot of zooplankton. This destroys the food supply of many fish that live in the area.

Sea jelly swarms have become a big problem for the fishing industry.

Some scientists believe the Australian spotted jellyfish is creating other problems, too. When hundreds of jellies live in the same area, they might damage the water itself. The jellies shed **mucus** from their bodies. This mucus could make the water too gooey for other animals to inhabit. Chemicals in the mucus might also poison the water.

LEARNING & INNOVATION SKILLS

Australian spotted jellyfish in the Gulf of Mexico have two unusual features. First, they are much larger than those in other parts of the world. Also, they do not have symbiotic algae living in their bodies. Without algae, they must obtain all of their food on their own. This makes them bigger eaters than their relatives in other parts of the world. How do you think this affects the fish and zooplankton populations in the Gulf compared to other regions? Think about why the jellies in the Gulf are so unusual. What other questions can you ask about these jellies?

CHAPTER FIVE

TRACKING THE INVADERS

Australian spotted jellyfish are clearly causing problems. Experts need to decide how to get the jellies under

Scientists all over the world are hard at work trying to solve the sea jelly problem.

control. But before people make plans to control the jellyfish, they must know what they are dealing with. Are there hundreds of jellyfish invaders or millions? Do they have any natural enemies? Why do they seem to disappear for years, then return by the thousands? How can they be controlled without harming other species?

Scientists must answer questions such as these before trying to control the jellies. Otherwise, they could waste time and money on poorly designed plans. They might even make the situation worse.

Unfortunately, these jellies pose problems that other animal invaders do not. For example, as polyps, they are almost impossible to detect. They are extremely small and hidden beneath the water's surface. There could be millions of them in an area and no one would know it. Little medusae can peel off and swim away before anyone knows the species has even invaded. This makes hunting for the polyps and young medusae almost impossible.

Some animal species can be controlled with poisoned bait. This method works only if the invader goes for the bait and the native species avoid it. If scientists poison the water where the jellyfish live, they will harm other animals living in the area.

Right now, experts are just trying to learn as much as they can about the jellyfish. In the Gulf of Mexico, for example, they are tracking the species' movements. This is not an easy task. The Gulf is an enormous area. Other invaded regions, such as the waters around Hawaii and the Philippines, are also very large. It takes many people to watch for the jellies in such large areas. To solve this problem, scientists are asking the public to help.

If you ever see a sea jelly on the beach, don't touch it!

One way that people help is by reporting jelly sightings to DockWatch. DockWatch is a program that relies on volunteers to gather information on jelly appearances. These volunteers walk along docks and beaches in Mississippi and Alabama. They count the jellies they see. They also check the water and air temperatures. They take notes about the wind speed and whether the water is murky or clear.

All of this information helps scientists better understand the jellies. In the future, it will help them plan the best way to get these invaders under control.

LIFE & CAREER SKILLS

DockWatch follows the movements of several different kinds of jellyfish. Some, such as the Australian spotted jellyfish, have only a mild sting. Others, such as the box jelly, have painful and sometimes deadly stings. Why is it especially important to track the movements of these dangerous species? Can you think of ways to keep people informed about these species?

Until scientists find a way to solve the problem, Australian spotted jellyfish will continue to cause trouble in their new homes.

CANADA

NORTH
AMERICA

California

UNITED STATES

Mississippi

South Carolina

Louisiana

Hawaii

Florida

Gulf of Mexico

Alabama

ATLANTIC
OCEAN

AFRICA

Puerto Rico

BRAZIL

PACIFIC
OCEAN

SOUTH
AMERICA

N
W   E
S

0   2000 mi
0   2000 km

This map shows where in the world Australian spotted jellyfish live naturally and where they have invaded.

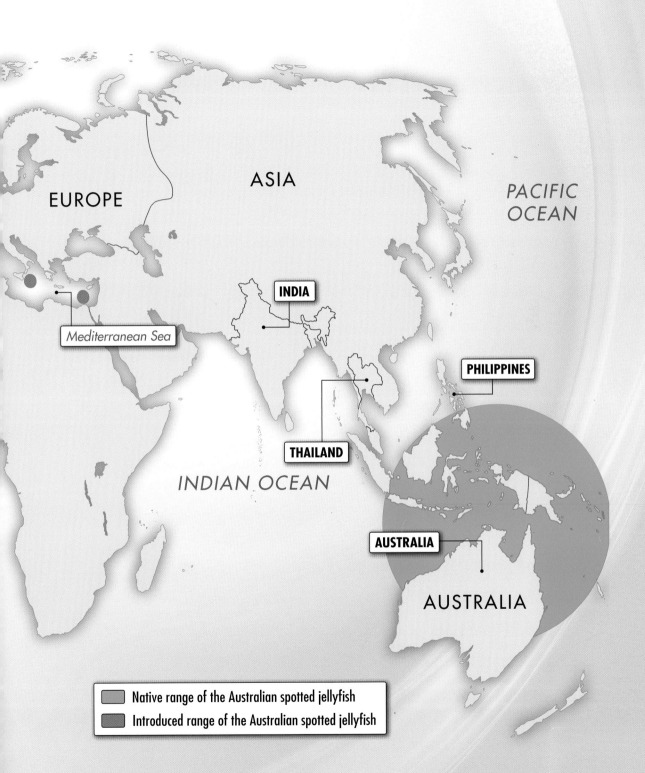

EUROPE

ASIA

PACIFIC OCEAN

Mediterranean Sea

INDIA

PHILIPPINES

THAILAND

INDIAN OCEAN

AUSTRALIA

AUSTRALIA

Native range of the Australian spotted jellyfish
Introduced range of the Australian spotted jellyfish

GLOSSARY

algae (AL-jee) simple aquatic organisms that are similar to plants, but have no true root system

anemones (uh-NEM-uh-neez) ocean animals with column-shaped bodies and many tentacles around their mouths

ballast (BAL-uhst) heavy material that helps make a vehicle stable

cnidarians (nye-DEHR-ee-unz) round, soft-bodied aquatic animals with stinging cells

fouled (FOWLD) dirty or clogged

invasive (in-VAY-siv) having moved into a new area and taken over

larva (LAR-vuh) the very young, undeveloped form of certain animals such as insects, fish, and sea jellies; the plural of this word is *larvae*

medusa (meh-DOO-suh) the swimming, umbrella-shaped form of some cnidarians; the plural of this word is *medusae*

mucus (MYOO-kuhss) thick, slimy material that is produced by the bodies of some animals

organisms (OR-guh-niz-uhmz) living things

polyp (PAH-lip) the non-swimming, stalk-like body form of cnidarians

prey (PRAY) animals that are hunted and eaten by other animals

species (SPEE-sheez) a particular type of plant or animal

symbiotic (sim-bee-AH-tik) describing a relationship in which two different species live closely together

zooplankton (ZO-plank-tuhn) very small aquatic animals that depend on water movements to carry them about

FIND OUT MORE

BOOKS

Cheshire, Gerard. *Jellyfish*. New York: Franklin Watts, 2008.

Coldiron, Deborah. *Jellyfish*. Edina, MN: ABDO Publishing, 2007.

Lunis, Natalie. *Gooey Jellyfish*. New York: Bearport Publishing, 2008.

WEB SITES

National Geographic—Australian Jellyfish Invade U.S. Waters

news.nationalgeographic.com/news/2007/08/070827-jellyfish-invasion.html

Read a story about the 2007 jellyfish invasion of the Gulf of Mexico.

Smithsonian Marine Station at Fort Pierce—Australian Spotted Jellyfish

www.sms.si.edu/IRLFieldGuide/Phyllo_punctat.htm

See photos and get information about the Australian spotted jellyfish from the Smithsonian Marine Station in Florida.

INDEX

ABOUT THE AUTHOR

Susan H. Gray has a master's degree in zoology. She has written more than 90 science and reference books for children and especially loves writing about animals. Susan also likes to garden and play the piano. She lives in Cabot, Arkansas, with her husband, Michael, and many pets.